THE BREATHLESS PAUSE

THE BREATHLESS PAUSE

Thoughts and Poems
by
Moyra Caldecott

Published by
Bladud Books

First published in 2007 by Bladud Books,
an imprint of Mushroom Publishing,
Bath, BA1 4EB, United Kingdom
www.mushroompublishing.com

All illustrations © Moyra Caldecott
Front cover: "The Tree of Life"
Back cover: "Mandala".

ISBN: 978-1-84319-552-8

Contents

THE UNIVERSE

Dare Darkness Grab Us

Shivering on a very small earth,
the night sky
formidable
with stars,
we pull the comforting blanket
of our love
over us,
and,
curled together,
dare Darkness grab us
and Time scatter us.

Full Moon

Sleeping
with the silver disk
of the full moon
on my forehead...
light shining
through the thick bone.
Watch how it glints
on mind-mirrors,
Scatters shadows,
and seeks at last,
the tiny seed-thought
that waits for birth.

New Moon

Seeing that hair-line
of flexed silver
in the frail green sky
of evening,
I exult.

God Watches Man

God watches man.
Man pulls earth shawl
around him
webbing himself with shadow.

Eclipse Of The Moon

The first men
witnessing
this bronze ball
rolling across the sky
must have feared
the vengeance of the gods.
But we,
in an Age of Science,
alone on this hill,
know better.
The stars are myriad,
but still the dark between them
unsettles us.
We who are dying
hope that Science
has left some secrets unresolved,
and, against all odds,
our death will be
among trumpets and cheering angels,
even our sins of omission
forgiven
by a smiling God.

The Hubble Telescope

The Hubble telescope
has changed my perception
of the universe.
When I look out
on a dark night
my mind sees
more than my eye...

Comet

A fist of cloud
limited to earth
hid
the giant traveller
from another galaxy.
And I
crouched
in my bed
surrounded
by small things
saw nothing of the splendour
of its journey
nor heard
its distant
thundering.

Black Hole

It was a shock
to realise
a black hole
was at the centre
of MY galaxy...
A spiralling wheel of light
being drawn into
a dense mystery
from which nothing can escape.
A black dot
as heavy as the earth,
a full stop
marking the end
of everything I know.

Binary Star

A white dwarf
and a neutron star
circle each other
every eleven minutes,
28,000 light years from earth.

Eleven minutes
while I talk to Rachel
on the phone.

Celestial Music

I read in the Scientific American
that scientists had discovered
the sun "rang like a bell",
constantly heaving with nuclear reactions,
and remembered the "celestial music of the spheres"
Medieval poets wrote about.
One evening of starlight
a friend played me a tape
of the sounds recorded
by one of the Voyager space probes
as it travelled the Universe...
Strange hummings and harmonies,
eerie and beguiling...

Today I heard
that the Kalahari San People
were asked by Laurens van der Post
what made them make music.
"Have you not heard the stars sing?"
They replied, puzzled.

On listening to astronomers speculate on the origins of the Universe...

Whether there is,
or is not,
a Multiverse
of which our vast Universe
is only a small part...
Whether a billion
mysterious singularities
exploded all on one day
or on others, at random...
Whether they are still exploding
as I drink my tea...
These questions
make my heart beat faster.
Beyond my front door
I see
a boundless
and magnificent
Infinity.

Under African Skies

I miss the stars
of Southern Africa
more than the land itself.
the Milky Way
a thousand times more bright
to my child's eye,
than this I see in old age
in the Northern Hemisphere.

Not dwarfed then, I,
but a giant
turning a great wheel of stars
around my head.
Now I have shrunk
and only a few stars
prick the darkness
of the sky.

Supernova: Crab Nebula
Photographing Memory

In 1054 a Chinese astronomer
observed a star exploding in the sky.
Today we have photographed
the filaments of gas and dust
that day the star thrust out
at thousands of kilometres per second.

But whether the floating debris,
the nebulous mist,
the pulsing neutron star
at its centre,
are still there,
we do not know.

The camera is not as subtle
as the mind
which can encompass
a multi-dimensional picture
of the explosion,
before and after
and to come...
The whence
and wherefore
and the why...

Galaxies

There are a thousand galaxies
in the constellation of Virgo
covering a region of at least
10 million light years across.
Billions more in the universe as a whole.
Giant vortices
and spirals of burning stars
driven by unimaginable forces...
Carried away by the expansion of space
through many dimensions...

And us —
with them.

Ring Nebula

In its death throes
an exploding star
pulses out energy,
gas and dust.
A red tide
engulfs
nearby stars and planets...
Travels outwards
swallowing
dark matter
and galaxies...
Rolling
inexorably
towards the Earth.

I shut my door
To keep it out.

Eternity

Eternity
cannot be measured
by the rotation
of stars.
It is measureless...
A point
where everything
is simultaneous
and has no beginning
and no end.

Proof

Astronomers calculate
the presence
of a celestial body
by noting
its influence
on those around it.

Why do we want
more proof than this
for the existence
of the divine?

Communication

If the two parts
of a split sub-atomic particle
can communicate
across great distances,
and human twins
can feel each other's pain,
it is quite clear
that we know very little
about how the real world works.

Betelgeuse

The supergiant star
Betelgeuse,
a thousand times the size
of our sun,
dominates the constellation Orion.

What planets
swing around
its vast furnace
waiting for extinction
when it goes supernova?

What child looks up
believing its sun
is a friendly one?

Joker

If the multi-verse
were a billion times the size
and the magnificence,
it would still be
only matter.
Why do we feel
there is a joker in the pack
that changes everything?

Saturn (The Roman name for Chronos — the god of Time)

Time swallows its children
regurgitating them
as dust.
So Saturn
whirls its rings
triumphantly...
All changed
and charged
with beauty...
Haloes of light
round a majestic planet.

Venus

We thought
the Greeks
chose so well
in naming their gods
that we
stole the names
for our planets.

Venus,
"The morning star",
is associated with the goddess
of Love and Beauty.
the seductress,
the mistress,
the lover.

Actually
the planet is
a hellish furnace
of volcanic activity,
constantly drizzling
deadly sulphur dioxide rain.

Mars

Mars —
a defeated warrior
deeply scarred and scored...
Scoured by mighty rivers
long since lost...
Stalked now
by dust devils
and red dust storms
planet wide.

We probe its surface
with long fingers.

Even a microbe found
would comfort us
who fear
to be alone.

Hereford Cathedral

Sun, Moon, and Stars
revolve in a fragment of Medieval glass,
a tribute to those scholars
in the twelfth century
who designed astrolabes
and played with cosmic numbers...
never dreaming
that their tentative steps
would one day lead man
to walk on the Moon
and discover other planets
orbiting other stars
in other galaxies.

NATURE AND PLACES
ON THE PLANET

While I was wasting the day

While I was wasting the day
the grass was growing,
daisies opening,
sunflowers
pushing up tall stems.

While I was wasting the day
the bee pushed its way
into a hundred foxgloves
and went home tired.

Now the light fades.
The rain wets my hair.
I smell honey-suckle and musk-rose
and take a deep breath
for tomorrow.

Spring

The whole green underworld is on the move.
Fists of bracken
rise for green power,
banners of tulip
proclaim the Sun's hour.
All stirring, whirring nature leaves
the ground
and pushes up
and out.

The forces of the City
in their dark towers
are under siege
and every concrete playground
has infiltrating green.
The buttercup sneaks up behind
the tarmac in the car park,
grass grows on roofs
and spilled Budgie seed
becomes a meadow on a window sill.

Praise be for such a revolution!
I'd fight with them
to topple every tower of faceless office down,
till every man
and woman, child,
had space on earth
to grow at least
one leaf.

Garden at evening

Out of darkening green
comes lupin light
and the blue flame of delphinium
and iris.

Roses fold light
into themselves,
petal on petal,
until the centre
glows.

Trees gather shadows
around them
like cloaks,
settling tired birds
into silence.

The moth shakes its wings.

I hold breath
hoping to see
the Presence I can feel...
catch the swish of feet
in the Long grass...
the brush of shoulder
against leaves.

A good day

London slides past.
I pick out the bits I want
and throw away the rest.
Everywhere I tread
diamonds spring up.

Dawn

When I looked out at dawn today
the clouds were threaded
with filaments of copper
and red gold.
As I turned my head away
and looked back again
a moment later,
the clouds were dull and grey.
How fast the glory fades...
but in that brief flush
it has lit the soul...
and, sometimes,
memory can replay it
when it is needed
on a dark day.

Spring in Cambridge

Spring in Cambridge
is all old stone
and new leaves...
Trees shaking off tired thoughts...
bud and bough rich
with sunlight and bird call.

Cambridge in Spring
is all bells
and choirs
ringing and singing...
willows like skeins
of green silk,
and lawns
so fine
only dreams
may walk of them.

King's College Chapel, Cambridge

Poised between dark and light,
between movement and stillness,
this is a moment of gathering,
of tension, before flight,
like a swan on a still lake
looking to the sky.

Then the chapel,
stone wings reaching,
tall neck stretching,
rises on song...
wheels over Cambridge
and soars out of sight.

Spring

Heavy we lie in the womb
And the earth's dark beginning stirs in us.
Sinews shoot with the flood bud of the spring,
And all the dark ways of light
Grow in our nerves.
This urge to sap and leaf is primeval
And the tall stones of the city
Have no word to say to it
Nor strength to hold it back.

Dawn

Ah lovely the dawn!
London turning towards the light...
bird song, like Haydn
and the last stars
clinging to the sky.
Creeping out of their holes
the early cleaners come,
the milkman
riding his chariot,
and the trains
bustling on the rails
almost empty
their windows bright rosaries
drawn through the fingers
of the trees.

Struggling from dreams
we flounder...
wondering.
Awake or not
we see visions...
glimpse truths...
wing
with the wild duck
that cries
between Brockwell and Dulwich.

London innocent
briefly.
life promising...
Death forgotten.

Monet's Water Garden, Giverny

Beneath the water
dark weeds and mud...
corms holding the future
coiled like springs.
Yet illusion
on this smooth surface
fools us all
suggesting
we may climb down ropes of willow
and find a world
the same
and not the same...
lilies of light
floating effortlessly,
and trees full of singing birds.

London

We have peeled back
the skin of the earth
and replaced its natural organs
with tar,
concrete
and metal.
The air
we have strung
with invisible beams
and waves.
We walk now
pulled
from every side —
by powers not our own —
strangely tense
and uncomfortable.

The motorway

Sunset blazing ahead of us...
storm clouds lurid
with cosmic fire...
heaven and hell
and all shades between...
The motorway runs
from London to Bath
a blade's width
between Life and Death...
what Is
and Might Be...
lorries and cars and vans
dodge and dive...
each decision
tugging at the Fate
of others...
each move
choreographed by one
affecting the many...
a ballet
where everything moves
simultaneously
and one mistake
can bring the curtain down
forever.

Bath

In summer
rainbow balloons
carrying the heirs
of the Winged Man,
King Bladud,
drift over these green hills...

In the valley
the hot waters of Sul
give relief
to the children
of a dysfunctional world.

Bath has always been
a potent place,
mingling people
from different cultures
and different realities,
the twin towers of the Abbey
crawling with angels,
and the streets
thronged with tourists
and ghosts.

The great red desert (between Bath and Bristol)

The skin of the land in this glade
is leaf mould
and crushed crystal
stitched by roots.
Above are fronds and leaves,
blue bells...
and trees
fretted by light and shade.

All is green and lush
and burgeoning...
life in a myriad forms
crawls and flies and hunts...
and I in the midst of this
stand still
listening to the cuckoo and the thrush.

But the sun burns in the sky
and underneath
the dark rich soil
the great red desert lies.
Strata of sandstone
bear witness
to ancient dunes,
to desolation and to death...

The planet turns
and so turn I.

Downside Abbey, Stratton on the Fosse

Angels are not to be trifled with.
Stone wings
delicately carved
in churches...
but in real life
swooping
when you don't expect them,
hiding
when you think you want them most,
listening to the words
behind the words you speak.
Angels do not grant wishes,
no matter how hard you plead.
They know better than you do
what you need.
Angels of this church,
please take care of my children
and their children
in the way you know best
and they need most.

Salisbury Spire

Heaven reaching spire...
cloud cutting...
star spearing...
Seen now
through a cloud of midges.
If only sharp words
and mean thoughts
had as short a life as they,
and I could stand
on this green earth
and reach to heaven
clean and clear...
pure heart
and spirit
honed to such a point.

Tree

The spread of this tree
out-domes St. Paul's...
Entering is initiation.
Leaving,
transformation.

The power of this tree
out-drives
man's ambition to the moon...
pumps life through every cell
and outlives history.

Without enmity
its strength
can crack mountains...
tumble cities...
Yet here it holds so still
and silent
that the frailest butterfly
is not afraid
to ride its shining leaves.

Tree — Wardour Castle, Wiltshire

Contained
in a web of light
this tree
showers
the sky with noisy birds
one moment,
and the next
is so silent
a heart beat
sounds like thunder.

The children
race around it
expending only a small part
of the energy
the tree expends
just standing still.

Fern leaved beech —
Botanical Gardens, Bath

This tree listened
when my husband died.
I leaned my head
against its trunk
and cried.
No words passed
but I took its strength
and knew
that life at last
secretly transforms
until what is seen
becomes unseen,
and what has been
is still to be.

Pine tree

I have always been wary
of a certain type of Pine tree.
We had three in our garden
in South Africa
and they dropped giant blue caterpillars
from their branches
every year.

One summer,
at Christmas,
I watched the branches bend and creak
in a menacing black wind
and then
a lightning whip-lash struck the tallest tree.
I saw it from the kitchen window
dissolve into yellow dust.
and fall, in slow motion, to the ground.
I did not mourn the tree,
but rejoiced that the caterpillars were dead.

The only trouble was
I developed a phobia against lightning
as well as caterpillars after that.

Bamboo grove

The bamboo
clustering together,
notched and rustling,
gives dark places
for children to hide.

We had a bamboo grove
in my garden
when I was a child
and I hid there
from predators
and enemies, imagined or real.

Sometimes I did not hear
my mother calling
because I was cowering
in my bamboo cage, walled in,
among ghost noises.

The asphodel lily

The asphodel lily
threads memories together.
Love flowers...
and dies.
Confronted with bare earth
I can't believe
life will flower again...
Yet, in that dark
and twisted corm,
many secret lives
are stored.

Brean Sands

Two people walking on wet sand...
their reflections
reaching down
to the dark roots of the earth.
I watch them in silence...
the landscape
and seascape
monochrome,
in different shades of grey.

A shaft of sunlight.
strikes the sea
in sudden silver.
The day becomes diamond.
The reflections of the two figures
appear now
more real than they.

Pear trees on a winter evening

Cut out
of the pale silk
of the sky...
a lacework
of holes
through which I see only darkness.

The Grey North Sea — Southwold, Suffolk

The grey North Sea
eats at this land
daily
swallowing houses —
tugging at the roots
of mighty trees
and toppling them.
Under the grey North Sea
lie land forests so ancient
they have turned to stone.
Not content with victory
the water
restlessly
turns and tumbles them,
breaking the crystal boughs
and fossil trunks,
transforming bark
to pebble
and resin to precious gem.

I pick up amber.

Transfixed —
flies
stare out blindly
at the sun
that shone last upon them
a million years ago.

Transformed —
the forest sings again
with bird song
and rustling leaves —
my heart
holding it
in triumph
against the grey North Sea.

Angels on the ceiling — Blythburgh and Southwold Churches, Suffolk

A ceiling full of angels —
worm eaten
in a wooden sky
replete with stars.
These Suffolk churches
lofty and light
still draw the mind
upwards
in spite of Cromwell's vandals
and neglect.
Winged messengers
of wood and stone,
brass and glass,
silently proclaim
an invisible host
we might do well
to call upon
in these dark times.

Tor: Dartmoor

At first I hear only wind
on this high Tor
wind in grass and heather
whistling through the rocks...
and then small voices...
thoughts of the ants
and the spiders
and the quiet crystals growing...
Listening...
the silence
is full of voices...
Beings
who have no names
and no place on our maps
speak
like wind through clouds
moving my thoughts
their way...

Listening to water at Dartmeet: Dartmoor

Water speaks
liquid tongued
language long lost
but lightly lilted,
telling each tale
a hundred ways
each
washed through other
and merging
to a new tale
told
all ways.
No way
man's tongue
can tell such tales
or see so many ways
of flowing words
through words
to tell true.

The conservatory in winter

Between the aloes and the icicles
a thin film of glass intrudes.
We sit upon cushions
among rubber plants,
eucalyptus and fuchsia,
snow falling,
light caught in the swords of ice
intensely.
The minutes fall softly,
lie white at our feet...
the glass intrudes.
We touch the hot flowers,
and thorns of ice draw blood.

We know illusions when we see them,
we feed on them
and they on us.
We know that if we name events
they happen in a different way
from things without a name.
We sit quiet.
our thoughts pricking the palms of our hands.

Summer

Summer
is opening my kitchen door
from a deep and monstrous night
to a garden
skimmering with sunlight.
and hung with ripe cherries.

Hyacinth

I breathe
the hyacinth...
not scent alone...
but colour
shape
and force...
the thrust of hyacinth
to sun...
the grip of hyacinth
to earth.

The school daffodil

The neighbourhood is full
of children carrying daffodils.
They are learning
about life.
In autumn they paid seven pence
for a bulb
and came home from school
clutching the rooty thing in their fists
sheathed in brown,
whiskered
and mysterious,
with a neat paper of instructions.
"Bury it," we said,
and into earthenware it went
with broken shards
and dank, mossy earth,
a few of last years leaves
and half an earthworm.
We put it in the cellar.
"Early darkness is necessary
for the secret ways of growth.
It has work to do
and must not be disturbed,"
we said.
The child looked every day
and saw nothing.
"It is slow, slow,"
we said,
"don't despair."
The child despaired.
But at Christmas
when the child had forgotten

we brought it up from the cellar
and showed
the small, pale,
naked,
elbow
of the first leaf.
"It's mine,"
the child said proudly
showing it to her brothers.
"How can it be yours,"
one said,
"it is living:
no living thing can be owned
by anyone but itself."
The child wept.
"It's mine,"
she whispered
and cherished it.

Two months the daffodil laboured
on our window sill.
We could never catch it doing it
but whenever we looked
it was bigger,
stronger,
greener.
Leaves proliferated,
buds unfurled
till on the sixth of March
yellow flags flying
green streamers blowing
out of every gate
the procession of daffodils
bearing children
triumphantly emerged.

Swan

Leaving the pond
and the gentle water weeds
a swan rode the ocean.
At first,
because it was evening
and mirror still,
not knowing
the fathoms
of deep and restless currents
stirring beneath
its poised white weight,
it rested easily,
on smooth silver.

But then —
slowly —
it began to feel
the pull and tug of the tide,
the unfamiliar hidden strength
and secret power of the sea.
No longer resting,
it rode the water
like a challenge,
rejoiced to feel
the primal rhythm coursing
in its own small veins.

No longer satisfied
with pools
of still water,
the swan rode on,
and never left the sea.

Florence — Summer 1980

The Laurentian Library

In this honey light
scholars hatched
the new world from the old...
dared heretic's fire
to bring us the machine.

Now that all the dark corners
are clear of demons
and the sky swept bare of angels
I wonder
if they did not turn one page too many
or perhaps
write one too few.

Florence

God is not here
in these dim churches.
He waits in the chestnut tree
to catch the tourist unawares...
springing on him
in the flicker of light
between leaves.
Those dead artists —
the best of them —
knew it
and always placed a tree,
or a lily,
or a landscape,
somewhere behind the solemn group
of protagonists
as a sly nod to the true pilgrim...

The Annunciation

Fro Fillippo Lippi
paints a young girl
being told that she is to give birth
to God
and catches
the grave attention,
the shy surprise...
the angel as friendly
as a sister.
How could she know, this child,
what it would mean —
and Fra Fillippo Lippi catches
this innocence,
this happy ignorance,
this pleasure
at the angel's glowing wings,
the lily
and the light...

But my heart aches for her
thankful it is not my own daughter
chosen to such a task.

Florence

There is something about shade
sifted through a hundred
thousand leaves
deep
in a Florentine siesta...
white sunlight
out there
on white stone
but here in the shade
dark
solid
pressing on the eyelids
behind which
all the day's beautiful churches
march
marble columned
holding space sacred
and whispering...

Saints

Saints caught in painters gold
beautiful
but making us forget
the dirt and flies
the pain
the cruelty
and the courage.
Those auras grew
on heads that had been stoned.
I would not dare
the things they dared
yet here I stand
and judge a colour or a line
as though they are pictures
of flowers
and not men.
These paintings are not ugly
enough
to give the rough truth
of what these men endured.
And I am grateful
the painters do not spoil
my Sunday afternoon
with too much reality.

Prayer to Horus — Egypt 1982

Let you wings be my wings
O Horus, the Sun's companion.
Teach me the currents of the air...
the high spiral
of the sky's heart...
the breathless pause
as the earth holds still
for the god to speak.

Fear has held my feet to the ground.
Fear has weighed me down.
My eyes and ears are blind and deaf with dust.
Immortal Bird
shake me free,
turn me loose
in your splendour...
Under your protection
let me soar,
Let me see the sun before its rising.
Let me see the world
at the point of transformation.

Dawn on the Nile

Mast threaded to the stars
this boat
silently in silence
glides,
darkness with its last breath
chilling our cheeks.

Even Time
is still.

A voice singing
silently in silence,
an ancient hymn...
opens the heart
to let the first light in.
Suddenly, with joy,
the sky is on the move with birds
and from the islands of ourselves
we greet each other.
Fish leap
and the boatman shakes out the sail.
Now the sun draws us home
along the gold thread
of the river...
and all
is festival.

The desert

The desert runs beside the river
like a hungry hound...
but spirit is held
in the hand of God
and cannot be touched
by the sand
and the storm...

The hermit

In this desert
sand blows to whim —
concealing and revealing
man's mighty works in stone.
Choosing to challenge it.
the hermit
sets his cell
and, bone thin,
drinks the blood-wine
of the sun-set,
eats the pale wafer
of the dawn.

From the mountains above the Valley of the Kings: Luxor

I climb these bare rocks —
the skeletal remains of time,
scorched clean by the sun
and picked by vultures...
On the summit
I face a sky
so darkly blue,
so vast,
my human heart stops beating
and the heart I use
is the earth's heart,
the breath I draw
is the sky's breath.
Beneath these mountains
lie the empty tombs of kings
and beside me on the rock
stand the pharaohs themselves
seeing what I,
as man,
can't see...
If I turn my head quickly
will I catch
the flash of a hawk's wing...
the breast of Isis...
Maat's numinous feather...?
All around me I can feel them —
but when I turn
I see nothing but dry, bleached stone
and the hot sky pressing down...

Grant, God of a million names,
that this moment
will stay with me
when the noisy town hits me
with a cloud of flies...
Grant, God who is beyond all names,
that I will know you
in the crowd.

Egyptian Mummy Room, British Museum. 15 July 1986

I wonder
if the spells they cast,
desperate to keep
their memories safe forever,
have played the cruel trick...
have held them back
from the shining realms...
pinned them to the earth.
The indignity of embalming
did nothing more
than imprison them in Time.
I feel their pain
their weariness
their disillusion...
What words should we say
over those sad and bandaged bodies
to send them on their way
when all the golden amulets,
the green heart scarabs,
and silver gods
have failed them?
Sometimes we ourselves
are released from suffering
when we tell a friend
our pain.
If we listen now
will our listening set them free?

Shall we tell them
that we understand
for we are they
and nothing in the human heart
has changed... will change...
though civilizations rise and fall
and even gods have different names...

Egyptian Gallery, British Museum

Do you hear them?
When I walk through this gallery
I sometimes hear their voices
like wind through dry leaves...
voices faded with the years
clamouring
to tell their tales...
bewildered
in this strange place...
confused and lonely.
There is no wholeness here...
no age old pattern into which they fit...
just broken bits and pieces...
a fist punches the air...
Here is the Queen's boat
no longer sailing
weightless among the stars
but earthed in stone
halved and abandoned.
On what shore does the lady walk
wringing her hands
and calling?
Is it her voice I hear
when
through a hole in Time
I catch the ancient sounds of Egypt?

The toads

From a gloss black pool
in a matt black night
gross toad noises
rise
in a great, rich,
sonorous roar,
a rumbustuous,
reverberating,
rumbling ricochet
of deep-throated
wart-bellied
sounds.

I crouch on the damp grass
and put my face
to within an inch of the water
anxious to see the minstrels
at their work.
But
a sudden mid-bellow silence
drops
like a guillotine.

Not a stir.

From the bland black water
bulging eyes
stare
back at me.

The Toads of Lake Titicaca

Robed
in magnificent folds
of beaded skin
the lords of Titicaca
sit portly now
upon
the ruins of Inca king
and concubine.
Pumping muscular legs
through the green weeds
"the bags that live in the marsh"
are the sole inheritors
of ancient splendours.

Theirs the last laugh.

The Sun King has long claimed
all else
But the sacrificial knife
missed
the joker in the reeds
when it glanced the shining waters of the lake
and took all that was rich,
and beautiful.

Storm

A shaft of light
pins a flag
of yellow grass upon a hill.
I stand
aware
of beauty...
responding to it
like a man striking gold.
Dust bowl
and shimmering rock
burgeon and are bounteous.
Then thunder-clap
turns landscape
inside out
and the underbelly of beauty shows...
black rust
and knotted shadow...
darkness
and clotted mud...
magnificent
and manifold.

Troy

The 'wine dark sea'
in Homer's *Iliad*
became reality for me
at sixteen
in Southern Africa.

At thirty six I dodged bees
in Agamemnon's tomb,
passed through the Lion Gate
and climbed to his citadel
in Greek Mycenae.
From there,
on a day of haze
and clarity,
I counted invisible warriors
embarking for the Trojan War.

In England, at seventy six,
I sat in darkness
to watch a film of Troy,
played by handsome actors
in Mexico,
the battle scenes
enhanced
by computer simulation.
Mythic illusion and allusion
so worked on me
that I watched, weeping,
as Achilles
dragged the body of Hector
behind his horse
around the walls of Troy.

When the last scene ended,
I stepped out into a street in Bath,
a city founded
by a descendent of a Trojan prince
and a Greek princess.
That night I saw on the television news
the body of an American soldier
(not played by an actor)
being dragged behind a car around the city of Baghdad.

Yosemite: Vernal Falls, 8 June 1979

No baptism more thorough
than the fall
of liquid crystal
in this rock font.
Sky giants
drown here.
Earth
is re-made
to shape the green heart
of this stone cleft.
Spirit drops to the abyss
slakes in the cold white swirl
and rises,
birthed in sunlight
and silver
to soar and sing.

Silbury Hill, Wiltshire — Sunday 16 April 1978

Far earth rim
rings me round...
earth pulse
beats
in my ears
with grass hush
and lark sound.

Lone
I watch
the sun watching
me...
I reach to it...
heart
still.

Sudden
my tiny hole
of vision
opens
to let the sky in...

Tumbled
by magnificence
I fall
to understanding
like a feather
to a whirlpool.

Cannon's Marsh, Bristol — Sunday morning
30 August 1981

Dockland on a Sunday morning
and Bristol bells
ripple and dance
touching the feet and the heart...
calling with urgent voices
the stray cat
and the woman far from home.
Cranes and yachts lie dormant
waiting for the day...
and in the quiet space
between the violence of the night
and the money-changing of the day
soul-thoughts grow
through cracks in the concrete...
soften iron rails...
shaft with sudden brilliance
through dark
and derelict places.

Sun in October

Sun in October
reminds me of Canaletto
touching everything into clarity,
separating each leaf
and tile,
making rough things fragile,
and all balanced delicately —
dependent
on light
alone.

SPECULATIONS AND MUSINGS

Eternal Life

No succession of days
eternal life.
No leaf fall
or harvest festival...
but a javelin
tipped with diamond
striking light...
the quick of the moment
with no extension
and no end.

The Christ

He will not come
as you expect,
swinging incense
and a Bible...
He will come
like a tiger from a field of daisies...
suddenly leaping
from the familiar
to the divine.

On Glastonbury Tor

On Glastonbury Tor
I thought
"This is a Holy Place."

Came the answer softly
like the slow flushing of sunlight.
across a clouded landscape...
"Anywhere
is a Holy Place
where is a Holy Thought."

I touch

I touch the sensitive point
from which all things spring...
and a running line of fire
spirals from it
faster than I can see,
burning the husks and stubble of my self
to clear the field
for the new planting.

Dreams

Dreams feed on sleep figments...
fragments
woven from one reality
to another,
creating a web
stronger than silk,
more fragile
than the spiders'.
Tossing and turning
the net tightens
around the psyche
until dawn breaks in,
and the new day
means more
than it did before.

On waking

Slick as quicksilver
the lizard of my dream
slithers
into the darkness
beneath
the rocks
even
as I reach for it.

I crouch...
moving sun surfaces
of stone...
knowing
I need to know
what that lizard
carried in its heart...

Stone
beneath stone
the lizard's secret home
evades
my grasp...
he watches me...
and I will have to learn
to lie quiet as sunlight
to tempt him out again.

Dreams

A patchwork of mist and sunlight...
dreams...
memories of the waking world
and dreams of dreams.
Images
that flit past
forming new shapes
even as you watch.
In this landscape,
familiar
and yet unfamiliar,
understanding
hovers
just out of frame,
too tenuous
to catch
and patch
into reality...
yet too significant
to ignore
as fantasy.

Insomnia

Trapped in a labyrinth
of thoughts...
Monsters everywhere...
not least because
I am
manufacturing shadows
where there are no shadows.

At last
I see a golden thread
of sunlight across the floor
and follow it
to where I believe
in myself again.

The wave breaking

The moment before a wave breaks
is my moment.
Once fallen
all poise and grace
is breath tumbled and jumbled,
one long rumble to the sand
and slow withdrawal into death.

But before
is all god and light.
Hope green with a green
that was before eyes crawled
from the sea to the land
and sprawled
to cover the earth with doubt
and with sight.

Quick as the whip of a wave
that is breaking
I am lost and locked
in a sea that has Time
for cell
and a jailer of rock.
Caught between action and thought
I am tied
to the shift of the sand
and the swift tug of the tides,
the drag of the long sea
and the swill and the swish that rides
the crumbling beach
and never lets me be.

Walking the ball

We walk disaster
like a circus dog, a ball.
The minutia of change
challenge us;
we adjust
the human heart to love,
to grief, to fear;
the body to city
war and peace...

The ball endures.
The dog
achieves his balance
and is gone.

Bird in a room

Wing beat against glass...
trapped
in a stale room...
lungs urge to the lovely air
that flies free in the wind.
Trees toss it about.
calling me
to breathe great gulps of it.

But the air I see
is held from me
by glass.
Smash as I will
my small and fearful heart
against its cold
I make no way.

'Lord, help me!'
The voice within me,
that is no bird's voice,
cries.

He lifts His hand to the catch
and I fly sudden free
arcing in light
that is the medium of the spirit
like bird to summer sky.

The cage

Sometimes trapped in my bird-cage self
I see the wind walking through the leaves
and all the bright people, free as air,
sifting through the sunlight
like dust turned to gold.
'Watch them', I say,
I cannot fly but in my cage
safe against the bully storm
I sing sweet madrigals.
Some day I'll hear a song from them
blown in on a gust of love.

Watch them, and see the gold of their bright lives
in bars about them, and from their feet,
a single chain as dainty as a lover's gift
and as heavy as a tomb.

Easter

I did not want
to stride straight
into the Presence of the Lord
carrying
the city on my back —
my hands dirty
and my pockets full of bills.

So I
rolled away the Rock
and sought Him
in the quiet.

I paused
with the change of light,
then picked my way
carefully
through the labyrinth
inside...

At the centre —
to my surprise —
I found the city
I had left behind.
'But where is God?'
I cried.
'Here,'
a voice answered
from the crowded streets
outside...

The dragon and the tiger

The dragon and the tiger
are legendary now
Both killed by man.
One used to ride
the high fine mountains of the mind,
the other
the glowing forests of the heart.

Where are they now
those golden
fearsome beasts?

Preserved in glass.

And in our blood
the gnat stalks
and the garbage fly...
all our loving small,
and our giving
tax deductible.

Visions come...

I say
I don't want to be in touch today
with those hidden worlds
inner worlds
deep
too deep
air rare
and rarefied
each breath
an effort.
But
ah!
visions come...
alien
and beautiful...
taking me home
to where the soul sings
and the heart soars
on golden wings.

A poetry reading in London

Look and see —
the poet speaks,
the faces close around him
folded inward
like flowers at night.
See how he dredges
from his secret store
words that stand him naked
in the light.
Watch those who quietly watch:
each one stalks alone
and carries in his pouch
a memory of his own.
The love that lies for him
with long white thighs
lies in the room in every eye
in different guise.
So sings the room with words,
the words not what they seem:
the images fall back to words
and back to the poet's dream.

Poetry Reading in Bath

A poet bares her soul...
words woven from her pain...
reading aloud
to a silent audience.
A mobile phone
intrudes
its silly jingle...
unstoppable
as the owner
flounders and flusters
in a duffle bag...
The poet waits.
The room waits.
The caller waits
doodling on a pad
in some other universe...
unaware
of the delicate thread of attention
she has broken.

On reading Henry Corbin: Mundus Imaginalis or The Imaginary and the Imaginal

There is a world we live in
not planetary
nor imaginary...
a world imperceptible to senses
yet sensible to the soul...
tangible to the heart
but not to the hand...
visible to the Being
but not to the man.
In this world we act
the ancient archetypes
and find meaning
where all seemed meaningless...
purpose
where all seemed purposeless.

My soul sees

Passing in and out of my body
my soul sees
what I do not see,
hears what I do not hear.
When he sings
the birds listen.
When he weeps
the Great Ocean
absorbs his tears.
When he teaches me,
I learn.
What perversity
makes me
want to stand alone —
a dry stick
breaking in the wind?

The Cosmic Conspiracy Theory

Doors that open
unexpectedly
into knowledge
you did not know
you were seeking.

Words
a friend says
that illuminate
a problem
she did not know you had.

Books that fall into your hand
from a shelf of thousands...
Road signs
read out of context...
Newspaper headlines
glimpsed over a shoulder
in a train
that transpose into something else...

Crop circles
made by hoaxers
unaware
from whence the inspiration comes...
Landscape zodiacs
and other mysteries
of ancient landscaping...

So many unknowns
in a world
we blunder through,
while the forces
that shape our lives
work
secretly.

Burned books

On an anniversary of a death
the Chinese write letters to the deceased
and burn them
believing that their messages will reach
the beloved
as the sparks rise,
as the smoke rises.

What if the Alexandrian library is not lost?
What if Emily Bronte's second novel burned by her sister
is not lost?
What if Gerard Manley Hopkin's poems burned as he
became a Jesuit, are not lost?

What if when we die
some ghostly part of us,
not limited by our language skills,
or eye-strain,
could read all we wanted
from the burned books,
and know all
that was ever known?

Interchange

The visible
and invisible
interchange
most curiously,
providing us
with many lives.
All capricious,
showing only in part.
No wonder
we so easily
lose our way.

The Archimedes Palimpsest

Text over text
inscribed,
millennia apart.
Faint markings
from Archimedes
only just showing through
a medieval monk's prayer
to his God.
Today we can read both.
Today we should not
throw one away,
but keep them as they are,
superimposed
and inextricably linked.
Maybe each text will reveal
more than the sum of its parts
if viewed together.

The Flat-lander

I love my friend,
but she is a 'flat-lander'.
She sees no mountains
if they are under cloud,
and sees no city
if it is under fog.
I, on the other hand,
live my life
in expectation
of hidden things...
prepared to ford a river
without knowing its depth.

Sometimes I flounder,
and nearly drown...
but sometimes
stepping stones appear
and I cross
to a marvellous country
full of angels and singing birds.

The moon caught in a tree

Wild the silver bird fought
the tree's black mesh.
Dazzle of feathers
as white fire sparked
in the flash
and the gleam of their fall.

The tree's blood-hold would not give.

The dark howled
with the wind's voice,
howled with the wound-pain
of the lonely traveller.
The lonely prisoner.

The tree strained,
creaked with the stress.
The cage of black and twisted sinews
could hold no longer...
Gave
to the sky
the mighty wings,
the celestial spirit.

All night long it soared,
rode,
the moon in its splendour,
mocking me
who mistook illusion
for reality.

The long vibration

Travelling as we do
uneasily
in this century...
seeking in city fumes
impossibly
the purity of sunlight
on elm leaves...
straining through traffic noise
for the slender sound of the lark...
We should be glad to know
that this moment
contains
the mysterious WORD of God
before it was spoken...
and the long vibration
that follows it.

Mayfly

It is odd
we feel so mighty
touching heaven from side to side
with outstretched thoughts.
Does the mayfly
presume
he knows as much
and feel so sure?

GORSEDD
(on making the writer an
Honorary Bard of Bath)

Today the storm
clears the air
of dross and dread.
Lightning flares,
burning off fear
and failure.
After the flood
the horn
hosts the gathering.
The drum beats.
The Druid lifts his arms.
The sacred grove arches over us
in green and glowing splendour.
I am held by roots
to a long line of word-smiths.
Sounds reverberate
against stone surfaces
carved with secret signs and sigils.
Words weave in and out,
stitching me to poets
long gone to earth
but still singing.

On reading a translation of the gospel of Mary Magdalene

Reading an ancient text
translated from the Greeks
to Coptic,
to French,
to English,
you would think
it reaches me
as "Chinese Whispers".
But mind sail
floats a seed
of meaning to me,
and in the compost of centuries
a plant takes root.
that flourished in Nile mud
two thousand years ago.

The Golden Arrow of Abaris

The golden arrow
of Abaris
flies yet.
It struck me in the heart.
thirty years ago
in a stone circle
in Scotland
when I thought I was dying,
and struck again
on Bladud's hill in Bath
when my husband was dying.

It flies between dimensions
carrying the secret equation
of Life and Death
in its golden tip
and shaft.
We can ride it
if we dare,
aware
that invisible worlds,
irrelevant
to Space and Time,
can change our lives
irrevocably
and without notice.

Writer's block

Years ago
insights came to me
as easily
as leaves
growing on a tree.
But then the autumn came
and the wind
blew them away.
I gathered what I could...
pressed them
between the pages
of my books.
Now I yearn
to grow more leaves.
Why is the Spring delayed?
I wish the one who nourished me
had stayed.

Glass drums

Talking with glass drums...
each word already broken
before it is heard.

I am left
with broken glass...
and the sound
of a ghost drum
inside the heart
that will not stop.

On hearing scientists talking and drifting off...

When 'the slow rolling scale of potentiality'
crosses the rising wave of probability,
sailing the sea of possibility,
drawing a map of predictability,
we stand amazed.
We weigh up the probable,
marvel at the possible,
rejoice at our potential
which is ultimately unpredictable.

Words

Three poets
argued about words.
A swan glided by.
The three fell silent.

The net of pearls

Reality is not a straight line
from past to future
through the present...
but a network
of inter-connections
going every which-way.
When we recognise
the nodes
sitting in a garden at dawn,
watching little finches,
or flowers opening,
a pearl is formed
and shines
even in the night
when we are lonely
and far from home.

On listening to a poet reading his own poem

Words spin and circle
like diamonds in a whirlpool.
I catch only some
and fill in the blanks
from my own source pool,
inventing my own poem
as the poet's words
pass by.
A kingfisher's wing
flashes in the sun
and dazzles me.
I pass out of understanding
into a region
of pure beauty
and coast in
on a different meaning.

Life story

Life is woven out of stories...
warp and weft
the threads interplay
and interact.

Mind stories
lying in bed at night
reshaping the day's events...
reading...
listening...
watching...
Stories shape and colour
the fabric of our dreams and memories.
Words and images
flux and flow...
change...
reform...
and give illusion
of reality.

Who can unpick the threads
and know
where we begin
or end?

On watching an artist at work

The sky emerges first
in transparencies of blue.
The tree
comes into existence next...
a firm image...
the wind already in its branches.
The ground takes shape
in various shades of dark,
hiding roots and bones.
We marvel at the creative act.
Two dimensions becoming many
as we watch.
The artist downs his pastel
and leaves
the page unfinished...
reminding us
there are still mysteries
unmanifest.

Multiple cross roads

All my life
I have played
with ideologies,
surfed heretical ideas,
picked my way
among the mine fields
of different religions.
I have found nothing
that totally satisfies me...
Not among the Scientists
who reduce life
to its smallest components.
Not among the "New Agers",
who base their philosophy
on gurus
and extra-terrestrials.
Not among the Evangelicals
who quote by rote
chapter and verse
from their holy book.
I stand, bewildered,
at multiple cross roads,
hesitant
to take the next step.

By the river at Batheaston

Slowly my tension
unravels
in this green place
with the dazzle of leaves
over water.
Maybe
I should not hunt
for answers...
but just drift,
like lovers in a boat,
through light...
through shade...
living the moment.

The present moment

This present moment
happens everywhere
simultaneously.

In outer space a star explodes.
An old woman on a garden seat
remembers the past
and fears the future.
An athlete wins a race,
a student graduates,
A suicide bomber
blows himself, and others, up.
Some lovers vow to love forever,
some do not.

An ant finds a path
for the collective.
A bee examines a flower.
A bird surveys
a prospective mate
from a roof top.
Bacteria and microbes
go about their business.
Cells divide.
Plants grow.
Cells die.
Minds lose their edge.
Will this present moment
be the point of transformation?
Or will it be just another moment?

Merlin

We shape the heroes of myth
each year afresh.
Merlin
has a different shape
for every one who says his name.
But somehow
there is still a shiver down the spine,
a glance over the shoulder,
when we think of him.
We're never sure the myth
is not reality
and Merlin might alight
from the next train
at our station
wielding powers
that defy analysis.

God's unimaginable spirit

Who can see
who sees us standing
in the world's traffic
the sudden flare
of God's unimaginable Spirit
in our souls?
And who sees
who sees an old woman with a basket
that she is a fire
that ever burns
and never is consumed?

Key secrets

Near or far
Time steals
our memories,
and thirty years ago
is as strange to me
as three thousand.
But sometimes
I catch a flash of wing
and remember
as though there were no break...
a kingfisher in the Drakensberg
and an ibis
in a temple on the Nile.
Time steals our memories
but in our hearts
key secrets lie
invulnerable.

I have no permanence…

I have no permanence
as the thought of God.
Tomorrow
He may not think me
as I am,
with name
and birthday
and little bag of tricks.

But That which is He
is Whole and not divided
and everything that Is
is He.

So in Him
my spirit rides eternally
like a drop of water
in the sea.

The mighty power of angels

The mighty power of angels
turns lead heart to gold.
The asking is the key...
the wanting...
reaching...
hoping.

Take now
this small and tarnished soul,
this creeping thing,
this dark and dormant seed...
Take it and fling it in the air
where the great rush of wings
will blow it
to heaven's gate
and there
so work its alchemy
it will a proud thing be...
a shining
and a free...

The spring goddess

At the wedding of Diana
and the Prince of Wales
there was dancing in the streets.
We passionately wanted a fairy tale
to come alive
and give magic and colour
to our drab and suffering world.
Even when the fairy tale went sour,
as the best of Anderson
and Grimm are wont to do,
we still clung to hope
that it would turn around.
Disappointed that she did not
give us what we wanted
we pursued her down a dark tunnel
like vengeful furies,
and killed her for her betrayal,
not of the prince,
but of us.
Then, horrified at what we'd done,
we wept and covered her with flowers,
hung ribbons from the trees in Hyde Park
as though she were a Spring Goddess.
I can still see the flowers...
millions of them...
(What a pity no one thought
to remove the plastic!)
During that week people saw shooting stars
and figures of her in the clouds.
Writing their eulogies
some people saw her ghost.

She was taken over water like King Arthur
and buried on an island of flowers...
The Spring Goddess we created
and destroyed
returned to the dust
from which we all are made.

Seven Poems on the Christ/Fish Acrostic

Vesica piscus

In the crossing of two circles...
the circle of God
and the circle of Man...
the Fish manifests itself.

The interpreter

I talk to the Fish
in my language
and He talks to me in His.

The interpreter
lives in a deep, quiet place
within me
and will not be hurried.

The language

This fish
speaks Hebrew,
and this one Greek.
I have heard
the murmuring of his voice
in Sanskrit
and found his symbol
on an ancient stone
carved
by a man
who had no tongue.

The sign

An old man
on the doorstep
draws the outline of a fish
in the dust.

The tall passer-by
pauses.
Recognition comes
to each
in its own clothing
of fire.

The wind blows the dust.
The fish loses shape.
But deep in the hearts
of the two men
the secret and eternal
message
swims on.

The rescue

There is a tidal bay
and when the moon pulls
the sea retreats
almost to the horizon.
The waters, with those who live in them,
go elsewhere,
and the sea-scape becomes a land-scape
Hurriedly the mud worms
take advantage.
The gulls swoop
and scream.

Looking for the shells
I squelch and stoop
and so it is
I come face to face
with a stranded fish
gasping in the unfamiliar medium of the air...

I hesitate.

The sea is a long way,
the mud flats difficult to walk upon
and if I go
I will certainly be late for tea.

He is nearly dead
'It can't be helped',
I think
And then...
and then...
I think of drowning
and I think of life
and I take him in my hand and run.

Covered in mud and aching in every limb,
at last
I fling him in the sea
that runs to welcome him.

And as I lie
gasping
the waters of the ocean
that gave him life
return to baptise me.

Rock pool

The eye of the pool
stares back at me,
its bland surface
reflecting
like polished metal.

I see myself.

Gradually
stillness
locks
the scene
and the pool eye
and this eye of mine
exchange focus.

I see the flowing weed
that forests the crannies of the rock,
the small creatures
whose universe this is...
anemones,
both flower and beast,
pursuing their natural way
with natural rhythm.

While He sees me
stripped of flesh and bone,
clad in memory
as long as Time,
flowing with a natural rhythm
through eternity.

We lean closer
and from the depths
where He has waited
long ages
swims the Fish.

The return of the fish

Darkly the dead waters
of the river
flow.
Debris catches
in the ruins of reeds,
strangles willow roots —
deforms all it touches.
poisons all who come to drink.

Years of forgetting
have done this.

I sit upon the bank
and look at the sludge
drifting past.

Someone calls...
And upstream
I see
work going on
to clear the stream.
Joyfully I run to help.

One morning
we see,
light gleaming on its scales,
a fish,
swimming...

WAR AND DEATH

Uneasy peace

All visions from the other side of time
pulse now within our darkening air.
We clutch them, pull them, stare
upon the flickering image of their line.

Isaiah come full circle shouts his doom.
The burden of his vision rides our dreams.
We throw his shadow on our screens
and entertain his ghost in every room.

Down fall the spires, the minarets,
the Senate House, the walls of steel!
Across the nerves war spins it reel
and flies the shrill insistence of its jets.

The splintering of the stone we cannot see,
the whisper of the end not hear:
all present tortures man must bear
upon the couches of psychiatry.

Too wide earth's fear

Too wide earth's fear, earth's pain —
I cannot hide before the hurricane.
The pestilent Bomb that crouches in our fields,
the sword avenging God above us wields,
the hate that festers in the blood of nations,
the sins of fathers on helpless generations,
all cry too loud.
Too thick earth's sorrows crowd.
I cannot weep the sea.
My tears are small, my sympathy
no larger than my heart.
I love only in part
and hate my enemies indifferently.
Earth herself her holocausts must weep.
I have my home, my child and sanity to keep.

The core

I wake with the old stale taste of yesterday
like myrrh still bitter in my mouth.
The dawn itself springs free
and light as mountain water.
Everything bounds and spins in brilliance.
Light hurls and whirls into a thousand shapes.
Only I, the hard dark core of this fantastic world,
remain heavy and immovable.

Christmas list

Dear Santa Claus
a warship please,
a guided missile
and a bomb:
perhaps some napalm
and a set
to liquidate
the turbo jet.
I think I'll have a radar screen,
a tube of germs
that can't be seen —
and if you've still got space you might
bring me a figure of Christ
to set alight.

Guided tours

Sodom, Pompeii, Hiroshima...
the guide speaks English.
It doesn't cost you much
if you take your own packed lunch.

This one suffered God's anger:
that was overwhelmed by natural forces;
the third was our gift.

See the pillar of salt!
(She should have waited for the guided tour.)
See the figures caught in stone,
screaming, clutching bags of gold
and one woman her child
(No one left in Pompeii
to close mouths and discreetly shutter eyes.)
Hiroshima
we can watch on television.
What a pretty cloud!
But we turn the channel when the close-ups come.

Hydrogen bomb 1958

In this
sour sweet death wish
of our age
we challenge God

Too long the centuries
of half deeds
and timorous crimes.
At a touch of a button
we will die
with the earth's
mackerel millions
blown about the air
like dust.

The coward

The ego is a coward
slinking down side roads,
avoiding eyes,
listening at keyholes,
gasping at what it hears.

Do you see
terrible letters cast by fire
on Belshazzer's wall?

The ego is a coward...
muttering incantations and formulae,
crossing itself with Geiger counters,
sipping the holy wine of neighbour's blood.

Thou shalt not...
and thou shalt not...

How many times the words
large as mushroom clouds...?
How many times a coward?

Toy soldier

I wore on my chest a silver medal,
on my shoulder an epaulette,
in my hand a gun.
They put me on display and sold me,
wound me up and said "Shoot!"

I shot.

Too late they found the toy soldier had a real gun.

Dawn

I love the return of the light —
the dawn —
the start of a new day —
the white page
unmarked —
the seminal thought
unexpressed.

Will this be the day
we'll be called to account
for all our other days?
Will this be the day
the world will mend its ways?

The old man on a garden seat

How many times the tigers quick as light.
spring from our trees.
While I, an old man on a garden seat,
see the sudden flicker of a leaf
and watch the massacre of bone, wing and beak,
the neat precision of the scimitar.

I sigh and wish the sparrows were not dead
and offer in their place, the tigers, bread.

The anniversary of a death

Trying to reconstruct a person
on the anniversary of his death
you must enter
the labyrinth of memory
with its twisting
and its turning,
its sudden shocks,
its false starts
and its blind alleys,
and its sudden revelations
of what you did not know you knew.

Someone emerges
from the shadows,
familiar,
yet unfamiliar...
substantial
yet unsubstantial.
Fading fast
leaving an ache behind...
and a question:
Did you ever really know him?

There is never enough time for love

Someone dies
and you say
you wish you'd spent
more time with her...
but you can't store time
to use in future years
when your heart aches.
What is gone,
is gone,
and you can never get it back
as it was... once...
on that perfect day.

Even memory
goes wandering
and never returns
to the same place twice...
but always mocks
with visions
nearly right,
but off precise.

One within the other

One within the other,
like Russian nesting dolls,
meanings
of each thought-event.
reveal themselves.

Gateway

There is a round hill
in the south of Bath,
off Mount Road,
that may well be
a gateway between the worlds.
On a clear day
you can see Glastonbury Tor
twenty miles away,
and the Bristol channel
gleaming red in the sunset.
On Good Friday Christians put crosses,
like Golgotha, on its summit.
Once I saw the great bronze ball
of the eclipsed moon
roll across the sky
from there,
and, another time, I counted
twenty-one hot air balloons
passing by...
strangers waving and shouting
as though we were long lost friends.

In Spring
it is clothed in May blossom
like a bride.

In November
my husband died
and I went there to watch him pass
into the other world...
disappearing into the autumn mists
like a legendary king.

LOVE AND FAMILY

First meeting

Fireside circle...
so quiet
you can hear the ash falling
silent as snow
in the dark places
on the heart.
No words...
No lights...
only dark paths
leading from one
to the other.
Will you take the first step
or shall I?
See
the fire is dying...
there is not much time
and the path leads into the unknown.

Dance

You know some desert spiders dance
around each other so
before they love or kill.
I've heard that, but I never knew
each step was so exacting,
each move that looked so free
was made against the strongest pull
of will compulsively withstanding lust.
Whether for death or love reacting
the same strange tension
tugs them back and drives them on
till finally the dust in sudden spasm whirls,
the tiny creatures lock
like giants in a monstrous love.

You know, it may be that I dread extinction
and so prolong the dance
with steps of such precise distinction.

Archaeologist

Excavate if you must
but leave one stone unlifted.
There may be nothing, less than dust,
but let it be my hope, my last retreat.
when you have ravaged through the rest.
Your spade may turn my fickle longings up,
may separate my loves:
may place each broken shard into another shape
and label it with dates and names,
your eye may search each battered coin
that once bought me my friends,
but when you reach the final stone
God help you if you don't
hold back just once
and let me be.

The body's Braille

Unlike the blind
we make our own dark.
Lying close
with organs sensitive to touch
we read each other.
The body's Braille
is easier than speech,
flows two ways,
the finger and the page
both take the message
and interpret it.

Thin skin

Do you get the feeling
that only a thin skin
separates you
from
the mob howling,
the broken hero,
the jackass laughing?
Warmly you lie
curled and enclosed.
Love tastes good.
But watch how you move.
One touch on the frail wall
that surrounds you
and the world will roar in on you
not caring
who it tramples.

Caught

Caught in the criss-cross clatter
of filament words...
the whole room a net of speaking...
webbed and tangled
and trapped in sound
I sit quiet, seeking
just once in the hub-bub to hear
Your heart ticking
like a pulse in my wrist.

Caught in the criss-cross webs
of the eyes of the room
I close my lids and hide
in the secret town behind them;
stalk in the alleys of my love
like a cat on heat
and not one of those prying eyes
accusingly do meet.

First snow

Are you not beautiful
day of snows?
Soft as feathers falling,
but with a killing edge.
Cover the harsh lines of our city
while you can.
Tomorrow
we will see it as it is
and weep.

The slow chisel

How many cold abstractions
disintegrate
with the close beat
of your pulse in mine.
This moment has no future.
It is poised
on a breaking wave.
Nor would I have it stilled,
locked in stone,
and broken
with the slow chisel
of Time.

Fog

The fog tonight is a Thing
spawned from the smouldering souls
of those on the verge of holocaust.
The city emanates its slithering, all-dimension Negative:
and there is no answer to the final question.

In the room my love flings the bed clothes ready
and the cold sheets warm to his limbs.

I ask no questions.

The chase

I fling my line deep as the sun,
fish as bright as pebbles foam and dart
but not one is worth the worm
that jiggles in the mud.
Golden skate and bream can be seduced
and die with ecstasy
but you in your corruption lie avoiding me.
The form of all things closes on your tail
but still you slip and scud
slither to avoid the hauling hand
the sliding rope and shadow of a sail.

Night sends me home,
land drags me in.
I throw the weapons of my trade away.

The fish that stalked for death all day
prepare to live.

Heraclitus said...

It's because Heraclitus said
everything's changing
everything's moving
that I need you to say you love me
over and over again.
This moment
caught in a flash of light
on a needle point
is lost
before I can grasp it...
and I am longing for you to come back
even before you are gone.

Must I...

Must I carry you always now?
I move fast with the crowd
keep them about me
laugh when they laugh
shout when they shout,
wear noise like a mask:
but all the time
I am somewhere else
in a quiet place
your touch on me,
enclosing me.

On too much self analysis

The psyche is a spinning top:
keeps only balance in the spin.
To bring a halt and turn within,
push shoulder to the coils of speed
and force dark corridors to lead
against the grain and deeper still,
demands for every twist a tighter will.
Each level bears a pressure more intense
till, shed of every normal sense,
each layer of the self discarded on the floor,
the ultimate is reached, the Core.
The final stillness of Negation.
No love, no hate, no obligation.

The psyche is a spinning top:
keeps only balance in the spin.

Thinking about you

Thinking about you,
Loudly,
In a concert...
Noise outside and inside
Clamouring...
Trombone screaming,
Tenor sax
Violent,
Words in my head,
You in my head,
Blazoned.
Accompanied by trumpets.

Suddenly the music cuts:
The hall is silent.
My mind skids
Too late braking its voice.
I look around,
Exposed,
Sure
That three thousand people
Now know my secret and
Unmanageable lust.

Wanting

In love there is no possession
only borrowing.
Two people pass through each other,
For a while
Inhabiting each other.
No one can say
Which one offers
and which accepts.
Neither hold.
They may stay so forever
Filling each other,
Image superimposed on image,
But they are two people
And nothing holds them together
But the wanting.

Hold tight

Hold tight,
make a fist
against the snow,
creep
into the palm of my hand...
Stay
covered
and curled
and warm...
my blood warming you...

Outside,
the big, big earth
is blanched
and transformed...
Hiding things...

Photographs

Perhaps all the time
I think I am with you,
you are somewhere else...
and I am sitting
in an empty house
with photographs.

FIVE POEMS ABOUT BIRTH

1. The planet

A star's inferno
first brought to be the embryonic earth.
With scum and steam the burning ball takes girth.
So crawl millennia of change away...
Time marked with drawn claw and brother's blood.
Horned, scaled and tusked our first proud parents
sink beneath the mud.
In stone they sleep who bear the destiny
of restless star in restless galaxy.

2. The courtship

Long light and love they watched the summer pass,
winged seeds shimmered in the breath of the sun.
'Easy' he said, 'easy for everyone.'
The silk air flowed,
warm limbs stirred the grass,
white light on water flickered
glass on glass.
Fish dived deep as ripples spun.
Nothing is easy.
Love gently begun,
crouched, holds something wild and harsh.
The earth may be a dark and quiet bed
to hold the lover as he lies,
but love
is not contained in still content,
it's bred of need.
Pain stalks beside
and loss shadows it.

3. The conception

One vagrant in a million drifting seed
found anchorage and stayed to make his home.
Big she grew, with his sweet summer blown.
Crawled from primeval mud the reptile needs
a million years for warmth of blood and bone,
but in her body
nine months alone.
The cord spins out,
the process speeds.
About her webs of sound and vision weave,
but she hears only within, the man unformed.
Her pulse responds.
The world is the child unborn.

4. The birth

Before a cataract the pool is still,
each leaf and twig awaits the sudden fall.
A strange unnatural calm suspends them all.
Then, caught by the undertow, they spill...
Splintered rocks reverberate, vultures call.
The woman catches at the sliding wall.
Her body bursts, her ancient cry is shrill.
Love is not easy, nor the ways of birth.
The first sun bore its child in fire and flood
and now each woman bears the burning earth
in wrack of bone and torturous gush of blood.

5. The parting

The Natural Law at certain times
contains concessions
to the human need for love,
and in his first blind months
the child has peace positive
within his small domain.
But stars fly ever out,
not one remains in all the restless universe.
Above,
a law decrees that all must change.
The circles widen, and intimacy done,
the two are hurled apart
while darkness chills against the bone.
Lost to each other in the spinning world
mother and child face holocaust alone.
Solitary they bear the destiny
of atoms hurtling to infinity.

You hear that?

You hear that?
That is the scratch of a rose branch
on the window pane,
the restless sliding itch
of thorn on glass,
infinite tiny nails
working on an irritant.

I sit silently,
and you cannot hear,
behind my silence,
the constant itch and scratch
of tiny nerves,
the twitch and rub of thoughts,
the restless drift and slide
of dreams.

This man I married

This man I married
thirty years ago
is more strange to me
than anyone I know...
as though,
standing so close,
we cannot see each other...

Time is a humming bird

At this moment
Time is a humming bird
and the moon a silver eye...
crystals grow...
flowers open...
And you and I...
Ah yes, you and I.

My three children

Three trees grow
rooted in the ball of earth
that is me.
Their roots twisting
around my heart,
penetrating my mind,
altering my vision,
my hearing,
my everything.
They are no longer saplings,
but have sturdy branches
that reach out across the world,
intertwined with others.
Yet I feel
everything they feel.
They hold me close,
renewing me with fallen leaves
and nutrients.
Without them
I believe
I would fall to dust.

After my husband died

Waiting for sleep
on a night when there is no sleep...
My husband beside me in the dark...
hand in my hand
from one world to the other.

The ones I love

This dark night
the planet turns
the ones I love
far from me.

Lord!
How my arms are stretched
trying
to encompass them.